Who Was
Milton Bradley?

D Who Was Milton Bradley?

by Kirsten Anderson

illustrated by Tim Foley

Grosset & Dunlap
An Imprint of Penguin Random House

GROSSET & DUNLAP
Penguin Young Readers Group
An Imprint of Penguin Random House LLC

Text copyright © 2016 by Kirsten Anderson. Illustrations copyright © 2016 by Penguin Random House LLC. All rights reserved. Published by Grosset & Dunlap, an imprint of Penguin Random House LLC, 345 Hudson Street, New York, New York 10014. GROSSET & DUNLAP is a trademark of Penguin Random House LLC. Printed in the USA.

Library of Congress Cataloging-in-Publication Data is available.

ISBN 9780448488479 (paperback)   10 9 8 7 6 5 4 3 2 1
ISBN 9780399542367 (library binding)   10 9 8 7 6 5 4 3 2 1

Contents

Who Was Milton Bradley?

One September evening in 1860, a young man stepped off a train in New York City. He had taken three trains to get there from Springfield, Massachusetts. Milton Bradley thought Springfield was a big city, but it was nothing compared to New York. The streets were crowded with people, horses, and carriages. Everyone seemed to be in a big hurry.

Twenty-three-year-old Milton noticed how the people were dressed. The women wore fancy hats with feathers and dresses trimmed in lace. The men wore tall hats and suits with shiny satin vests.

Milton thought they looked like they were all wearing their Sunday best—and it wasn't even Sunday! But he hadn't come all the way to New York City to admire the fashions. He was there to convince people to buy and play a game.

The next morning, Milton bought a new hat and suit so he would fit in with the New Yorkers. Then he took a few samples of his game and walked into a stationery store. The store sold paper, pencils, and pens, plus small games and toys. He found the manager.

"How do you do, sir? I am Milton Bradley of the Milton Bradley Company of Springfield. I have come to New York with some samples of a new and most amazing game, sir . . ."

Milton showed the man The Checkered Game of Life. He explained how players moved across the red-and-white checkered board, making both good and bad choices about life. He said that people who loved games would find it entertaining. People who usually thought games were a waste of time would find it educational.

After sitting down with Milton and playing the game, the store manager bought all of Milton's sample games. Milton returned to his hotel to pick up more. He brought samples to a different store. They bought them all. In only two days, Milton sold the hundreds of games he had brought with him.

Milton was thrilled and proud. He had believed that people would see themselves in The Checkered Game of Life. And he had been right. Milton was only twenty-four years old when he decided to put all his energy into becoming a game maker.

Over 150 years later, people are still playing games created by the Milton Bradley Company. And The Game of Life is one of the most popular board games of all time.

CHAPTER 1
Two Apples Plus Four Apples

Milton Bradley was born on November 8, 1836, in Vienna, Maine. His parents were Lewis and Fannie Bradley. Lewis was a carpenter and a factory worker.

The Bradleys never had much money, but they were a close, happy family. They were very religious. They went to church on Sundays and did not drink, dance, go to the theater, or gamble. But they believed in having other kinds of fun. They spent their evenings reading together and playing games like checkers or chess.

Milton's parents were very involved in his education. When Milton was still quite young, he didn't understand how to add or subtract. Lewis put six bright red apples on the kitchen table.

He asked Milton to count them. Milton counted
six. Then Lewis took away two apples. He asked
Milton to count them now. Milton counted four.
Lewis put back the two apples. Now there were
six again.

Checkers

Checkers is one of the world's oldest known games. Boards that look like checkerboards have been found in ancient ruins in Mesopotamia (now Iraq and Kuwait). Scientists have dated them back to 3000 BC. An Egyptian version of the game, using a twenty-five-square board, dates from 1400 BC.

In AD 1100, French players began playing on the sixty-four-square checkerboard we use today. In England, the game was known as "draughts" (say: drafts), but Americans have always called it checkers. The first checkers championship was held in 1847 in Scotland.

Suddenly, Milton understood—the numbers in the math problem in front of him represented real things that you could count, put together, or take away. Using the shiny apples made all the difference for him. He thought this was a wonderful way to learn. Milton always remembered how his father helped him understand math by using apples.

When Milton was eleven years old, the family moved to Lowell, Massachusetts, so Lewis could take a job in a cotton factory. Milton attended the Lowell Grammar School and immediately became best friends with a boy named George Tapley. Milton was a serious boy. George was happy and cheerful. He could always make Milton laugh. They were a perfect pair.

Milton had a talent for drawing and decided that he would study art at the Lawrence Scientific School when he finished high school. Milton didn't have enough money for Lawrence when he graduated from high school, so he went to work.

He got a job in the office of a draftsman—a person who drew plans to build machines.

Milton earned extra money by taking a job selling paper, pens, and ink. Lowell was famous for its busy factories, and many people traveled far from home to find work there. That meant they all wanted to write letters home as often as they could.

At night, Milton went to the boardinghouses where the factory workers lived, asking if anyone wanted to buy paper and pens. Milton was very successful. He wrote in his diary that the female factory workers bought more from him than the other salesmen because they thought he was funny and clever.

The Lawrence Scientific School

In 1855, Milton finally had the $300 he needed to attend the Lawrence Scientific School. But when his two-year art course was nearly finished, Milton's father found a better job in Hartford, Connecticut. Milton reluctantly left school and moved to Hartford with his parents.

But there weren't any jobs for him in Hartford. Milton wanted to do *something*—even if he didn't know exactly what yet. Milton decided to try his luck in a bigger city: Springfield, Massachusetts.

CHAPTER 2
Springfield

Milton arrived in Springfield on a warm June day in 1856. He had just one bag that held his clothes and the lunch his mother had packed for him. Milton needed a job and a place to live. Near the railroad station, he saw a sign for the Wason Car-Manufacturing Company. They made train cars.

While drawing plans to build machines in Lowell, Milton had learned a lot about being a draftsman. Maybe the railcar company needed one.

A manager at the Wason Company asked Milton if he could draw a locomotive, the main car that pulls the train. Milton said he was sure he could. He didn't mention that he had never even been on a train before his trip that morning!

The manager gave him some paper and pencils. Milton saw pictures of locomotive parts hanging on the walls of the room. He based his own drawings on them.

When the manager looked at his work, he offered Milton a job. Milton gladly accepted, then celebrated by buying a five-cent glass of lemonade.

Milton lived in a boardinghouse at first. But when another Wason employee offered to rent him a room in his house, Milton was happy to move. While Milton lived there, he met the sister-in-law of his coworker, who was visiting from Boston. Her name was Vilona Eaton.

Vilona Eaton

Milton and Vilona fell in love and wanted to get married. But first Milton had to earn enough money to support a wife and family.

That was not so easy. The Wason Company factory closed in the summer of 1858, and Milton was out of work. But Milton was confident. He decided that it was time to go into business himself.

Milton rented an office in Springfield in September 1858. He put up a shiny new sign that said "MILTON BRADLEY, Mechanical Draftsman & Patent Solicitor." He would

draw plans for making machines and also help people get patents for their inventions. Sure, business was bad all over the country, but people weren't going to stop making or inventing things, were they?

Patents

A patent grants the rights to a particular invention to the inventor. It guarantees that the inventor is the only person who can make or sell that invention. A patent is a kind of protection that allows people to brand or trademark their invention, so everyone knows who created it.

A patent request must be filed with the US Patent Office. Along with the application, the patent office asked inventors to include a drawing of their invention. Inventors who couldn't draw well enough often hired an artist or draftsman to make the drawing for them.

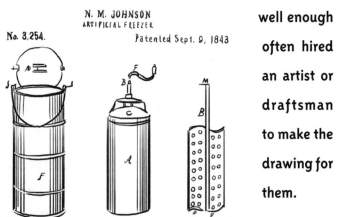

N. M. JOHNSON
ARTIFICIAL FREEZER

No. 3,254.

Patented Sept. 9, 1843

Milton smiled at his sign, then went back into his office. He sat down at his brand-new desk and waited for customers to start coming in. But no one came.

People didn't seem to have the money to make new machines or to develop new inventions. Milton began to worry. He had used most of his savings to start his business. He was running out of money.

Then Milton got lucky. The Pasha of Egypt—
a man of very high rank—placed a huge order
for train cars with the Wason Company, and
the factory re-opened. The Pasha had requested
an extra-special car for his personal use. The
managers at Wason asked Milton to draw the
plans for the fancy car. Milton was able to buy a
diamond engagement ring for Vilona!

The Wason Company gave Milton a framed print of his drawing of the special train car. Milton was intrigued by the picture. It had been created using lithography—a fairly new form of printing. Milton had an idea. He could open a print shop and start a lithography business!

CHAPTER 3
Let's Play a Game

Milton's old friend George Tapley worked for a company in Rhode Island that also printed lithographs. Milton visited George and learned everything he could about printing. After two weeks of studying, he bought a printing press and went back to Springfield.

In May 1860, Milton put a new sign outside his office on Main Street. This one said "MILTON BRADLEY CO, Publishers, Lithographers."

Business was good. But by late summer, things began to slow down. In the United States, the Northern states and the Southern states were divided over the issue of slavery. Many people feared there might be a war. They were too worried to spend money. They weren't interested in expanding their companies. Business seemed to be slow throughout the country.

The 1860 Presidential Election

In 1860, the United States of America was a divided nation. Most Northerners wanted a president who would outlaw slavery in any new states. Slave-owning Southerners wanted slavery to be legal in new states. They threatened to secede, or break away, from the United States if an antislavery president was elected. People worried about the country splitting apart.

The Democratic Party itself was divided. The Northern Democrats nominated Stephen A. Douglas for president. He thought voters in each state should decide whether they wanted slavery or not. Southern Democrats nominated John C. Breckinridge, who supported slavery.

Stephen A. Douglas

The very new Republican party nominated a little-known Illinois lawyer named Abraham Lincoln. He had spoken out against slavery, but he also felt it was important that the whole nation stay united.

John C. Breckinridge

Even though Lincoln had no support from the Southern states, on Tuesday, November 6, he won the election. Seven Southern states seceded from the United States before Lincoln was even inaugurated. A month later, the first shots of the Civil War were fired.

Milton was frustrated. He still hadn't earned enough money to marry Vilona. But he didn't have any ideas. He was becoming depressed.

By this time, George Tapley had moved to Springfield. He invited Milton to come over to his house for a visit. He wanted to cheer Milton up.

George had financial problems, too, but he didn't worry as much as Milton. At George's house, the two friends played an old English game on a board with oval playing pieces. Milton loved it.

Suddenly Milton had an idea. Why couldn't he invent a board game? He already owned a printing press. He could print the game himself!

Milton tried to think of a game that all kinds of people would like. Many serious people didn't believe in playing games. They thought they were a waste of time. But what if a game could teach you something while you had fun playing it? Milton went home and thought about what kind of game would be exciting to play yet still be satisfying to people who didn't approve of games.

He knew that he could print the board design in his own shop, so he wanted to create something unique. A game that only *he* could sell.

Milton came up with a game that taught players about both the good and not-so-good aspects of life. The board had sixty-four red and white squares. The red squares were blank. The white squares had words printed on them. Some squares represented positive things, like "Happiness," "Success," "Bravery," and "Truth." Others squares had negative ideas, like "Crime," "Prison," and "Disgrace." Players turned a spinner to see how many squares to move on the board. They chose which direction to go. The goal was to earn points from the good squares and end on the "Happy Old Age" square instead of "Ruin." Milton named it

"The Checkered Game of Life." The board was checkered—broken into squares just like a checkerboard. And real life was checkered—including both the good and the bad.

It took Milton a week to create a version of the game with which he was completely happy. Then he showed the game to George. He thought it was funny that Milton, who was usually  so serious, had spent so much time developing a game. But when George played The Checkered Game of Life, he liked it, too. It turned out that the normally serious Milton Bradley was very good at making a fun game!

Milton and his assistant worked twelve hours a day, six days a week. They cut and printed each board, and they made the pieces and spinners themselves. They assembled several hundred games. Now Milton just needed to sell them.

He knew he would need to travel to a bigger
city that had a lot of stores. Milton decided to take
his games to New York City. He worked with his
assistant to pack up the hundreds of game boxes
he had designed and built.

And Milton's trip to New York was a big success. He sold The Checkered Game of Life to stationery stores, department stores, and even newsstands. After all the games were sold, he had one more thing to do: He wrote to Vilona and asked her to choose a day for their wedding.

CHAPTER 4
Entertaining the Troops

Milton returned to Springfield, but did not go right back to making games. The presidential election was less than two months away. Milton hoped that Abraham Lincoln would win the election. Milton, like Lincoln, was against slavery. Many other people in the Springfield

area also supported Lincoln. Milton made thousands of prints of a photo of Lincoln looking handsome and clean-shaven. Because people were excited about the election, Milton sold a lot of the Lincoln portraits. Then he left Springfield to marry Vilona in Boston. Their wedding was on November 8, his twenty-fourth birthday.

After Lincoln won the election, an angry man walked into Milton's office. He complained that the prints didn't look like Lincoln at all! He showed Milton a new photograph of President Lincoln with a beard. People were no longer interested in the portrait of a beardless Lincoln. They wanted to see the president the way he looked after his inauguration. Some people even demanded their money back. Sadly, Milton lost a lot of money on the Lincoln prints.

Lincoln's Whiskers

In October 1860, an eleven-year-old girl named Grace Bedell from Westfield, New York, wrote a letter to Abraham Lincoln. She told him that she wanted him to become president, but she thought he "would look a great deal better" with whiskers.

She thought it might make more people vote for him. Lincoln wrote her back and thanked her for the idea, but said he'd never had a beard and didn't think he could change now.

But then he decided to grow one anyway! A few months later, after being elected the sixteenth president of the United States, Lincoln visited Westfield. He asked to meet Grace. He told her that he had been growing a beard for months, just for her. Today in Westfield, New York, there is a statue showing President Abraham Lincoln meeting young Grace Bedell.

But Milton didn't worry too much about his beardless Lincoln portrait. He was saved by The Checkered Game of Life. Because the game had sold well in the New York City stores, news about it spread throughout the Northeast. Milton got orders for the game from stores all over the state of New York, then Boston and other parts of New England.

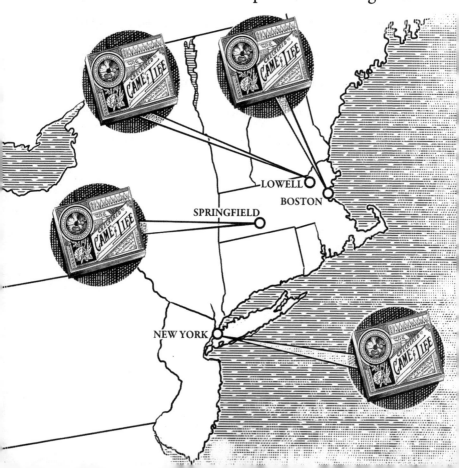

LOWELL

BOSTON

SPRINGFIELD

NEW YORK

Milton and his assistant worked hard to keep up with the orders. They printed, cut, and put together forty thousand copies of the game during the winter of 1860–61.

When the Civil War began in April 1861, the local military unit asked Milton to help draft plans for new types of weapons. Suddenly his patent business took off. Everyone seemed to have an idea for a new invention that could be used in the war, and they all needed illustrations of their ideas for patent applications. Milton spent his mornings drawing plans for his customers, then spent his afternoons and nights working on plans for guns and other weapons.

Milton had really wanted to join the Union Army. But the army commander in Springfield wouldn't let him. He told Milton that designing the new guns was the most important job he could be doing. Milton understood. But he wished he could do more.

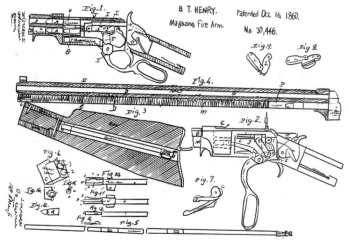

One day Milton walked by a group of soldiers at a nearby camp. They were standing around fires, trying to keep warm on the cold fall day. Milton thought they looked sad and bored. He realized that soldiers didn't have much to do when they weren't marching or fighting.

Milton believed that fun was important. He even thought it might help people get through hard times. How could he help the soldiers have a little bit of fun?

A Soldier's Life

When the Civil War began in April 1861, there were very few full-time soldiers. The Union (Northern) and Confederate (Southern) Armies were almost all volunteers who had left their homes and jobs to fight. They were farmers, storekeepers, carpenters, and blacksmiths. They didn't know how to be soldiers, so they lived in camps where they were trained. They practiced marching together and shooting on command.

Some learned how to operate cannons. They all had to learn to obey orders from their officers.

The soldiers spent most of their days training and cleaning equipment, such as cannons and guns. When their work was done, they didn't have much to do. They waited until it was time to march off to the battlefield or to their next camp. That was the life of the Civil War soldier.

Milton came up with a small pocket-size game board and tiny pieces that could be used to play nine different games: chess, checkers, backgammon, five types of dominoes, and of course, The Checkered Game of Life. He called his new game set the Game Kit for Soldiers.

Milton handed out the game kits to local soldiers. Then he wrote to the stores that had already been selling The Checkered Game of Life and told them about the new Game Kit for Soldiers. He was selling them for a dollar each.

Soon Milton got as many orders as he could handle. Many were from charities that bought large numbers of the game to give away to soldiers. Milton had found his own special way to help the Union soldiers—by helping them pass the time and giving them a small way to have fun.

CHAPTER 5
All in the Cards

Milton struggled to keep up with all the orders for the soldiers' kits and for The Checkered Game of Life. To make each game, he had to print the picture of the playing field. Next he created the board by cutting a stiff square of cardboard. He pasted each picture onto each board.

Milton also had to cut out every piece the players used to move around the board as well as the cardboard spinners. Then it all had to be packaged into a box. It was a lot of work! Finally Milton found an assistant who could take over most of the printing and cutting. Now he had more time for creating new games.

Milton's next game was a pack of cards called "Modern Hieroglyphics, or Picture Writings for the Times." Hieroglyphics were an ancient Egyptian form of writing that

used pictures. "Writings for the Times" meant that the puzzles were about current events. Instead of using ancient hieroglyphics, Milton used a rebus to spell out words and phrases on each card.

What Is a Rebus?

A rebus is a puzzle that
uses a mix of pictures,
letters, and numbers
to spell out words
and sentences. For
example, a picture
of an eye, a heart, and

the letter *U* is a rebus that spells out "I love you."
Rebuses are related to pictograms, an early form of
writing, where pictures represented words. Today
rebuses appear in the way we write text messages
and use emoji: "U R GR8" or

The rebus puzzle cards were a huge success, but that created a problem for Milton: He had to keep inventing more puzzles. Luckily, the game's fans came to the rescue. They started to send Milton their own puzzle ideas. Milton used the best ones in new packs of cards. And he sent each contributor a payment for their puzzle.

Milton wanted people to have fun with his games, but he also hoped they could learn something. His next pack of cards focused on history. "Patriot Heroes, or Who's Traitor?" had an image of a military leader from US history on each card. Players won points by correctly identifying

the person on the picture. Milton liked to keep his cards up to date, so he even included generals who were fighting at the time in the Civil War.

By 1864 the Milton Bradley Company was too busy for Milton to handle with just one or two assistants. Milton asked George Tapley if he would like to join him and be responsible for running the office and the factory while Milton developed new games.

But George was busy working for a newspaper publisher. He didn't join the Milton Bradley Company. Instead he loaned Milton $10,000 to help it grow. He suggested that his brother J. F. Tapley and his business partner Clark Bryan handle the business for Milton.

That sounded fine to Milton. He liked being successful, but he really just wanted to invent games.

CHAPTER 6
Moving Toys

The Civil War ended in 1865, and the United States struggled to recover from the devastating war. Many businesses were in trouble. But the Milton Bradley Company managed to keep going.

Although people didn't have much money, they wanted to have fun. Board games didn't cost that much, and it could be used over and over again to entertain a whole group of people. Milton and Vilona themselves often had fifteen to twenty people over to their house to play games. So Milton Bradley games kept selling, and Milton kept making new ones.

In 1866, Milton studied a toy drum he had ordered from Germany. It had pictures painted on the side. As Milton turned it around and around, he came up with an idea.

Milton printed a series of pictures on a long roll of paper. The paper was glued onto a cylinder and set in a box. A person turned a crank to transfer the paper from one cylinder onto another. As the paper unspooled, the pictures rolled past a window in the box. Milton decorated each box to look like a small stage.

A lamp could be placed behind the paper so the pictures would be lit like a stage in a real theater. The box also included tickets and a poster, to make it seem like an actual play. Milton included a script so that one person could be the narrator and explain the story the pictures told of the Civil War. Milton wrote the script himself. He put in plenty of facts, but also made sure there were jokes to entertain his customers. Milton named his toy the Myriopticon.

People loved it. Families and friends gathered in parlors, pulled the curtains shut, and lit the

Myriopticon with a lamp. Then they watched and listened to the story. They played it over and over again.

Milton was now fascinated by the idea of moving picture toys. Milton made one called the Zoetrope, or Wheel of Life. His pictures showed figures doing simple movements, like chopping wood, running a hurdle

Have you seen this wonderful and amusing Instrument?
Published by Milton Bradley & Co.
Springfield, Mass.
For Sale Everywhere.

race, or flying on a trapeze. It was a big hit. The Zoetrope is now considered one of the earliest forms of a motion picture.

Not all of Milton's games were played indoors. Croquet, a French lawn game, had become popular in the United States. Players set up wickets—small metal arches—on their lawns. Then they used mallets, or clubs, to try to hit wooden balls through the series of wickets.

However, no one played by a standard set of rules. And many people used homemade versions of clubs and wickets.

Milton wrote his own simple version of croquet rules and had them patented in 1866. He began to manufacture croquet sets. By 1867, Milton Bradley croquet rules and sets were everywhere. Milton loved croquet himself and continued to create new versions of the game. He made a set with smaller clubs for children and a light, portable one for families to take with them when they traveled. Croquet remained a popular outdoor game for decades.

How the Zoetrope Worked

The Zoetrope was an open-top drum with vertical slits in the side that created the illusion of movement using still pictures.

- A roll of paper, printed with pictures showing a figure in various stages of movement, was placed inside the bottom of a small drum.

- The viewer looked through a slit—the viewing holes—on the outside of the top of the drum and spun the Zoetrope.

- The entire drum spun around to reveal each picture.

- When the pictures, each showing the next motion in a series of tiny movements, quickly passed by, the effect was as if the figure was animated.

The faster the Zoetrope turned, the smoother and faster the figure in the picture moved.

In 1867, a very different kind of game became popular all over the United States. "The Terrible Fifteen Puzzle" was a handheld flat square with sixteen spaces for small square tiles. It came with fifteen tiles in place, leaving one space empty. The tiles had numbers

on them, but they were out of order. The object was to put the numbers in order from one to fifteen. The empty space created room to move the tiles.

The puzzle drove people crazy. Everyone wanted to solve it. Newspapers wrote stories about it. One man playing the puzzle on a ferry boat grew so frustrated he threw it in the water— then tried to dive in after it!

The Milton Bradley Company began to produce its own version. Milton didn't like the word "Terrible" in the name, though. He named his puzzle "The Mystic Fifteen Puzzle." It was a big hit.

The Rubik's Cube Craze

The Terrible Fifteen hasn't been the only puzzle that everyone wanted to solve.

The Rubik's Cube was invented in 1974 by a Hungarian professor named Erno Rubik. He first created a cube out of small wooden blocks. Each block was colored red, blue, green, yellow, orange, or white.

Rubik then tried to solve the puzzle by twisting the blocks into place so that each side of the cube would show only one color. It took him a month to do it!

In 1980, Rubik's Cubes began to appear in stores around the world. People quickly became fascinated by the cube. Millions were sold. There were stories about the Rubik's Cube in newspapers and on television.

Today there are Rubik's Cube speed-solving competitions. In 2014, a robot made out of LEGO bricks and a smartphone solved it 3.253 seconds!

The Milton Bradley Company was very busy in 1867. They were making many games by then. The business was doing well. Milton was not concerned with the company's success. He was worried about his wife.

Vilona had been ill for the past year. And in March 1867, she died. Milton was devastated. He was thirty-one years old and alone. For weeks he couldn't work. He went on long walks to fill his lonely days.

Finally, he asked his parents to come live with him in Springfield. Milton even gave his father a job at the Milton Bradley Company. With his mother and father close by, Milton began to feel better. He began to think about games again.

CHAPTER 7
Toys for Learning

Milton went back to making games, but he also became interested in something else—education. A music teacher in Springfield introduced him to the ideas of a German man named Friedrich Froebel, who talked about something called "kindergarten."

Friedrich Froebel

Most schools in the 1800s focused on learning through memorizing facts and numbers, but Froebel thought that children learned better by playing. He also believed that children could learn at a very young age. Froebel started "kindergartens," or classes for children as young as five years old. (*Kindergarten* means "children's garden" in German.) Kindergarten students played games and sang songs. They learned to build, count, add, and subtract by using different colored blocks, balls, sticks, and rings.

Milton thought these ideas made sense. He wondered if the Milton Bradley Company should start making the blocks and other toys to be used in kindergartens. But the men who ran the business disagreed. They thought the Milton Bradley Company should just stick with games.

Milton's good friend George Tapley and his wife, Mary, worried about Milton being lonely. They kept introducing him to some of their other friends in the hope that he would fall in love and remarry. Milton was always polite, but wasn't really interested. He was busy with his work.

One day Milton visited the Tapley house and a young woman named Nellie Thayer was there.

She was planning to become a teacher. Milton thought Nellie was intelligent and beautiful. They talked for hours. They began to spend time together. Milton even taught her how to play croquet. They became engaged on Christmas Eve and married in May 1869. They moved into a new house, and Milton's parents stayed in his old house.

Milton and Nellie were just settling into married life when he heard that Elizabeth Peabody, a teacher from Boston, was coming to Springfield. She was giving a lecture about kindergartens. Milton and his father went to listen to her.

Elizabeth Peabody's stories about how her students enjoyed learning captured Milton's imagination. Milton and his father agreed that the new kindergarten way of teaching was a lot like the way Mr. Bradley had taught Milton when he was a boy. And Milton thought that was the right way to learn. He decided that his company would start making the blocks and balls and other things Friedrich Froebel said kindergarten students needed to learn.

Elizabeth Peabody (1804—1894)

Elizabeth Peabody was born in Billerica, Massachusetts. She was a brilliant student and teacher who was interested in new and different ideas about education. Elizabeth also wrote several books and ran a bookstore.

Elizabeth opened her own kindergarten in Boston in 1860. In 1867, she went to Germany to study other kindergarten classes. When she returned, she began to promote the idea of kindergarten as a standard of early learning. She wrote guides for teaching kindergartners and helped start training schools for kindergarten teachers. By the 1880s, there were over four hundred kindergartens in the United States. Elizabeth Peabody is considered one of the leaders of the kindergarten movement in America.

The business managers of the company weren't happy about these ideas. They just wanted to keep making games and weren't interested in expanding the company to make educational blocks and toys. But Milton didn't care about that. He cared about changing children's lives for the better.

The Milton Bradley Company was growing. In 1868, it had moved from Main Street to a bigger building on Bliss Street. And in 1870, they moved to an even bigger five-story building on Harrison Avenue. Milton's family was growing, too.

His first daughter, Florence, was born on June 22, 1874. Milton was thrilled, but also sad. His mother had died right before Florence was born. He and Nellie invited Milton's father to come live with them and baby Florence.

Milton's business partners, J. F. Tapley and Clark Bryan, grew nervous about all the time and effort Milton put into making blocks and toys for kindergartens. They were inexpensive so that teachers could afford them, but they didn't make much money for the company. In 1878, J. F. Tapley and Clark Bryan announced that they were leaving the company. But George Tapley disagreed. He told Milton that he should stick with the kindergarten products that he believed in.

Later that same year, George agreed to join the Milton Bradley Company. Finally, the two lifelong friends would be working together.

George owned four buildings on Cross Street in Springfield. The company moved into George's buildings.

The Bradleys' second daughter, Lillian Alice, was born on January 13, 1881. There wasn't yet a kindergarten in Springfield, but Milton and Nellie used Froebel's ideas to teach their daughters. Sometimes the girls even helped Milton come up with new ideas.

One day Milton found Florence struggling to memorize multiplication tables. Milton told her to bring some friends over to the house. When Florence returned with her friends, Milton gave each girl three toothpicks. He asked each girl how many she had. Then he showed them how three times two girls made six toothpicks, and three times three girls combined for nine toothpicks.

The girls understood, and Milton had a new idea. The company began to make "multiplication sticks," brightly colored sticks that helped students make groups for multiplying numbers.

Milton and Nellie had guests over for dinner almost every night. Often the guests included Massachusetts teachers, principals, and school superintendents. They wanted to learn more about the educational products Milton was making. He wanted to hear about new ideas in schools and the growth of kindergartens.

Milton thought about all the other things teachers needed in kindergartens. He had always believed that bright colors were important for the games he made. He thought color mattered to children, too. The company began to make crayons, watercolor paints, and colored paper.

Kindergartens became more colorful places. And
teachers had much more useful tools with which
to teach.

CHAPTER 8
The Education Department

In 1889, Milton decided that the family needed more room. The Bradleys moved to a larger house. Nellie's parents moved in with them as well. The new house was perfect for parties.

There were sliding doors between rooms that could be pushed aside to make even bigger rooms. The crowd at the Bradley house almost always ended up playing parlor games.

Milton was an enthusiastic game player. He loved joking with his guests and seeing them have fun.

Parlor Games

What did people do for entertainment before TV, movies, video games, and the Internet? During the 1800s, people often gathered together and played parlor games. The *parlor* is what we now call the living room. These were games that could be played indoors by a large group of people. Some games involved activities, such as charades, where a person acts something out and the rest of the group has to guess what it is. Others were word games, such as Consequences, where players create a story by saying a word or phrase that the next person has to use to continue the tale. A nineteenth-century party would never have been complete without a few spirited rounds of parlor games!

Milton always encouraged people to bring ideas for new games and test them out at his house. If he liked a game, he paid the person who had contributed the idea, and the Milton Bradley Company manufactured it. One game that came out of the Bradley parlor was "Kerion," a game where players raced pieces around the board to see who could get back to the beginning first. Another was "Happy Days in Old New England," a game where players landed on spaces marked with old-fashioned New England activities, like sledding and making maple-sugar candy.

During the 1800s, the Milton Bradley Company made toys as well as board games. It introduced a toy Buffalo Bill Gun, named after the popular traveling show Buffalo Bill's Wild West. The gun was so popular that stores were sold out of them as fast as the factory could make them.

Jigsaw puzzles were also big sellers. Many puzzles showed maps, famous places, or pretty scenes. But Milton had a different idea: He wanted to create a puzzle with some action. He drew a picture of a train wreck, and the factory made it into a puzzle called "The Smashed Up Locomotive."

Kids loved it, and it became the company's best-selling puzzle up to that time. Milton followed that with "The Blown Up Steamer," a picture puzzle of an exploding fire engine. Milton knew what kids liked.

The company added new buildings in 1887 and 1891. It now had separate departments for education, games, and publishing. Milton spent most of his time with the education department. His father had died in 1890, and Milton knew how important education had been to him. It was important to Milton as well.

Milton always wanted to keep his employees happy. He sometimes threw company parties, where everyone gathered together at tables set up in one of the factories and ate dinner together. And it was not uncommon for the workers to play with the games and toys. After all, someone had to test them out.

Milton went to the factory every day. He worked in the morning and took a nap every afternoon. But he couldn't sleep if there was too much noise in the factory, so the machines were turned off during his nap time.

By the end of the nineteenth century, the Milton Bradley Company made desks, chairs, tables, chalkboards, paper, paints, and educational toys and games—almost everything a school needed. His business managers had once wanted Milton to stop spending so much time on the education department because it wasn't as successful as the games division of the company. But those days were now in the past. Educational products were now every bit as profitable as anything else the Milton Bradley Company produced. Milton had been right all along: Quality supplies for teachers were good for business.

CHAPTER 9
Going Home

In 1896, Milton built a vacation home on Casco Bay in Maine, the state where he had been born. He named the cottage "Shore Acres." He and Nellie spent as much time there as they could. Milton liked to sail and go for long walks. He started painting with watercolors. And of course, he and Nellie had guests over almost every night. Their parties usually ended with a round of games.

Milton was now a wealthy man, but he never cared that much about money. He, Nellie, and the girls had enough to live comfortably, and that was all Milton had ever really wanted. He didn't buy a big mansion or fancy clothes, or take expensive trips to Europe. He liked riding around Springfield with Nellie in one of the new automobiles, but that was his only luxury. In many ways, he was very much like the Milton who grew up in Maine. He believed in working hard, going to church, and staying close to your family. He believed that learning was important. He also thought that fun was important. And he knew that both of those things could be combined.

Milton retired from the Milton Bradley Company in 1907. George Tapley took over all the departments and ran the entire company. Milton and Nellie divided their time between Massachusetts and Maine. Florence married a young man who went to work for the Milton Bradley Company. Lillian married a chemistry teacher. Milton was happy to be a grandfather to his three grandchildren.

Milton died on May 30, 1911, after a short illness. He was seventy-five years old. The company managed to stay in business through the hard times of the Great Depression, and its manufacturing of fighter airplane parts during World War II helped it grow. After the war,

Americans once again had money and time for games. The Milton Bradley Company created many new games that became popular in the 1950s and '60s, like Battleship, Candy Land, and Twister. In 1960, they created a one-hundredth anniversary version of The Checkered Game of Life, called simply The Game of Life.

The Milton Bradley Company began to make electronic games and video games in the 1970s and '80s. In 1984, the company was bought by Hasbro, a large game and toy maker. Hasbro also bought Parker Brothers, one of Milton Bradley's biggest rivals. Hasbro still makes Milton Bradley educational-activity toys and games.

Back in 1910, the employees of the Milton Bradley Company had given Milton a book they had made especially for him. It was called *Milton Bradley, A Successful Man*. It told the story of the first fifty years of the Milton Bradley Company.

The Game of Life

The version of The Game of Life made in 1960 was very different from the 1860 one. The 1960 game included pieces that looked like tiny cars.

Players had to make decisions about things like buying insurance, playing the stock market, and borrowing money. They earned money based on their jobs and could win extra money by landing on special spaces. The goal of the game was to finish as a "millionaire" or "tycoon." That's a big change from the simple "Happy Old Age" of the original.

Now there are video-game versions of The Game of Life, and there are The Game of Life apps for phones and tablets. In 2010, the game was inducted into the National Toy Hall of Fame, 150 years after Milton sold his first copy.

Milton Bradley and his company were indeed successful. The company had survived hard times and made many popular games. It had made Milton famous and earned him plenty of money. But Milton thought he was successful for other reasons. In a 1902 issue of *The Kindergarten Review*, Milton wrote that success did not mean to him "the glitter of gold or the glamour of . . . fame." Instead, he wrote about how satisfied he was that he had helped with the kindergarten movement in the United States. He said he was proud that he had stuck with making education products, even when other people said it was a bad idea. But he knew it was a good idea. He knew learning could be fun. And if there was one thing Milton Bradley knew about, it was how to have fun.

Timeline of Milton Bradley's Life

1836	Born November 8 in Vienna, Maine
1854	Graduates high school
	Trains as mechanical draftsman
1856	Hired by the Wason Car-Manufacturing Company, to work as draftsman for locomotives
1858	Wason Company closes
	Starts own business as draftsman and patent solicitor
1860	Gets idea for The Checkered Game of Life while playing games with friend George Tapley
	Marries Vilona Eaton
1861	Creates Game Kit for Soldiers
1866	Invents the Myriopticon, panorama toy that tells the history of the Civil War
	Starts selling the first mass-produced croquet sets
	Produces the Zoetrope, a moving-picture toy
1867	Produces The Mystic Fifteen Puzzle
1869	Marries Ellen "Nellie" Thayer
1874	Daughter Florence is born on June 22
1881	Daughter Lillian Alice is born on January 13
1898	Introduces eight-color box of Bradley wax crayons
1907	Retires from company
1911	Dies in Springfield, Massachusetts

Timeline of the World

1836	The Battle of the Alamo is fought in Texas
1839	SS *Great Western* becomes the first ship to cross the Atlantic using only steam power
1844	The first telegram is sent
1849	The safety pin is invented
1852	Elisha Otis introduces the first elevator with a safety system
1861	The American Civil War begins
1865	President Abraham Lincoln is assassinated
1872	Yellowstone National Park is established
1879	Thomas Edison makes the first long-lasting incandescent lightbulb
1881	The gunfight at the O.K. Corral takes place in Tombstone, Arizona
1883	The Brooklyn Bridge opens
1889	A massive flood destroys Johnstown, Pennsylvania
1891	Dr. James Naismith creates the game of basketball
1897	*Dracula*, by Bram Stoker, is published
1903	The first modern World Series is played
1909	Fingerprints are first used to solve a murder case
1911	The first Indianapolis 500 auto race takes place
1913	The crossword puzzle is introduced

Bibliography

Lepore, Jill. "The Meaning of Life." *New Yorker*, May 21, 2007.

"Milton Bradley." Playground Professionals. http://www.
playgroundprofessionals.com/encyclopedia/m/milton-bradley.

Shea, James J., and Charles Mercer. *It's All in the Game*. New York:
G. P. Putnam and Sons, 1960.

*Skeers, Linda. *History Makers: Toy Makers*. New York: Lucent Books,
2004.

Whitehill, Bruce. "American Games: A Historical Perspective." The Big Game
Hunter. http://thebiggamehunter.com/main-menu-bar/history/
american-games-a-historical-perspective/.

Whitehill, Bruce. *Games: American Boxed Games and Their Makers
1822–1992*. Radnor, PA: Wallace-Homestead Book Company, 1992.